The Staff of Merricat's Castle Nursery School

Gretchen Buchenholz, Director
Susan Faldetta
Debbie Padills Fernandez
Jane Look
Patricia Luby
Janet May
Christine McKenna
Patricia McKenna
Debbie Morenzi
Margaret Morrison
Rosa Negron
Tracy Rambo
Mary Ann Sullivan
Chris Antoneck-Taylor
Joan Weitzman
Linda Mattariello Wosczyk

Teach Your Child with Games

By Gretchen Buchenholz
and The Staff of Merricat's Castle Nursery School

Edited by Manon Tingue
Illustrated and designed by Leora M. Sies
Introduction by Bruce Buchenholz, M.D.

A FIRESIDE BOOK
Published by Simon & Schuster, Inc.
New York

Copyright © 1984 by Gretchen Buchenholz and Manon Tingue
All rights reserved
including the right of reproduction
in whole or in part in any form
Published by Simon & Schuster, Inc.
Simon & Schuster Building
Rockefeller Center
1230 Avenue of the Americas
New York, New York 10020
FIRESIDE and colophon are registered trademarks of Simon & Schuster, Inc.
Designed by Leora M. Sies
Manufactured in the United States of America
Printed and bound by Halliday Lithograph
1 2 3 4 5 6 7 8 9 10
Library of Congress Cataloging in Publication Data
Buchenholz, Gretchen.
    Teach your child with games

    "A Fireside book."
    1. Educational games.   I. Tingue, Manon.   II. Merri-
cat's Castle Nursery School.   III. Title.
LB1140.35.E36B83   1983   372.13′078   84-1229
ISBN: 0-671-47464-2

Dedication

This book is dedicated to Norman the Rabbit. Since Norman is not greatly impressed by what we have to say, it is more fitting dedication to give him this opportunity to speak for himself:

Almost all nursery schools have animals. They are rarely heard from. The greatest contribution of this book is humanity's opportunity to hear from me. The nursery school where I live and work has been the whole of my life. No one could be more steeped in his or her subject.

Some years ago I became aware that after my children played with me for a while they invariably drifted off and became engrossed in other things. Naturally, I had to ask myself what could be more alluring than I. So I watched very carefully to see what they were doing. Apparently they felt drawn to leave me in order to take part in some rituals. They lined up in formations; they went through certain weird motions. They used things that I guessed were extensions of themselves. Why?

At first I thought I had stumbled across a religious rite. (After all, they would only leave me for a higher call.) Then I observed some levity that seemed inconsistent with that conclusion. (Rabbits don't need levity.)

Gradually I began to perceive that these ritualized behaviors were responsible for some salutary changes that were taking place in my children. Namely, as time went on the children became more and more rabbitlike. They had less trouble getting along with each other, were less frequently upset, and gained a measure of equanimity. They even seemed partially to overcome their most curious lack—self-confidence. Those observations showed me that these rituals support growth and learning.

I am sure my children would benefit if the people who collect and keep them for me in the interim between schooltimes also became aware of the basis for these rituals. Whereas the insights are, of course, mine, the rest of the staff has, in these pages, described certain "games" (the technical word for these rites) that are the most useful in dealing with issues that are exclusively human—the fear of helplessness and the need to establish a sense of self.

Naturally, my understanding is purely intellectual. It comes about through genius rather than empathy, since rabbits don't have these problems.

Norman the Rabbit

Contents

Like children, games start on an elementary, simplistic level and move to higher levels as more skills are acquired. However, it's important to remember that all children develop at an individual rate of speed—some fast, some slow—but like the turtle in the race, they get there in the end and it doesn't matter when.

Throughout the book, whenever the pronoun he *is used read* he/she *and whenever* mother *is used read* mother/father. *We acknowledge and laud the consistently stronger roles fathers play in bringing up their children.*

Introduction

Most of us tend to think of such things as fun, play, pleasure, and games as frivolous pastimes. We are likely to contrast "fun and games" with the serious business of living. Children, on the other hand, seem to know that playing is worthy of serious attention. We must have known it too when we were very young, but somehow we've forgotten and so we've created a dichotomy between play and work; between "for fun" and "for real." This book hopes to show parents that children's fun is "for real."

It's perfectly obvious that children take pleasure in playing. They play whenever they can—not because they are children and inadequate for the real responsibilities of life, but because playing *is* a real responsibility of life. It's the one real responsibility of life that they meet better than we do. And they are smart enough to stick to what they do best. Children are people who are "becoming," and the games they play are the work of becoming. Each section of this book explains how this work is done.

Call it mastering, skill development, problem solving (if it gets too rowdy it can be called a lot of other names); there is a method in the madness of each game children play. Children, by virtue of being children, have limited strengths in every area. The younger the child, the more helpless he or she is. It's an adult's world, and even the least observant young child sees that he's much smaller and less able to cope than most people. He may not express this awareness directly but he certainly plays hard at coping.

Most of us have a pretty strong sense of "being." We know very well *that* we are and we have a reasonable feel for *who* we are. This sense, this awareness derives from experience and is the sense of "I am the one to whom this is happening," or "I am the one who is making this happen." It's important to keep in mind that children don't have this clear and strong sense of self. Their games are the happenings that help bring this sense about. A child who is "It" in a game of tag is the focus of concentrated attention and thereby gets strong affirmation of his or her self. A child who can build a tower of blocks sees that he or she "can" and therefore must "be."

Anyone aware of these small persons—outnumbered and outsized, not quite sure who or what they are, having a lot of coping to do—must be impressed by the courage and faith that allows them so joyfully, enthusiastically, and energetically to do their job of play. This awareness makes us more respectful and understanding of the games children play, games that are ingeniously contrived to meet their needs.

Bruce Buchenholz, M.D.

Game Categories

Games are divided into four broad developmental categories. All of them overlap. It is, for instance, often impossible to develop a "basic skill" without "imagination." But we hope that these categories will serve parents as a general guide to the myriad ways in which their child progresses toward knowledge and control of self.

The first category is *Games for the Imagination*. These are literally mind expanders. Imagination, including fantasy, is the way the child manages to put the world at his feet; it transforms the mundane into the glorious. Give the child a box—he makes it his castle; a collection of rocks may become his private cliff dwelling and an empty carton his office. His imagination is an expression of his curiosity and assumptions about the world around him. It is a special gift of the child's own spirit that makes it possible for him to use anything he encounters for games of the imagination.

In the field of education, the term *Basic Skills* refers to the skills necessary to read, write, and compute. Each of these disciplines requires the development and coordination of a complex group of interacting capacities. For example, before a child can begin to learn to read, he needs some degree of directional orientation, a basic body of facts, some development of visual discrimination, and the ability to symbolize.

It is important to know about the need for basic skills so that we can avoid the grave but common error of encouraging the child to read before he is ready. A parent whose focus is on teaching his child to read early is missing the point and doing a disservice to the child. A major aspect of reading readiness is the acquisition of basic skills, and the most effective way to teach a child to read is to help him gain those *prereading skills appropriate to his level of maturation.*

Motor Skills games are useful in the development of large-muscle control and coordination. They are a prime outlet for energy and when used with music introduce the child to the experience of rhythm. The child crawls before he can walk, walks before he can run, runs before he can hop, and each of these is a giant leap forward. Games which involve these skills can also be found in the team-games category, since these are often a form of gait game as well.

Team/Group games enhance the child's social development, and playing them is one of the ways children develop meaningful relationships with others. When he starts out, the child has a limited ability to cooperate or collaborate. By the time he is five he has acquired the sophistication to understand his role on his team. Relationship games help the child overcome his fear of isolation and loneliness.

A final note: it's important to realize that though these games are broken up into three age groups, many of them are still applicable to children who are younger as well as older. A younger child who has a particularly well-developed skill will be able to enjoy a more advanced game that utilizes that ability. On the other hand, an older child may enjoy the familiar and successful sensation of playing a game he's known for a while and is quite good at.

In either case, the pleasure experienced by the child when involved in these games is invaluable.

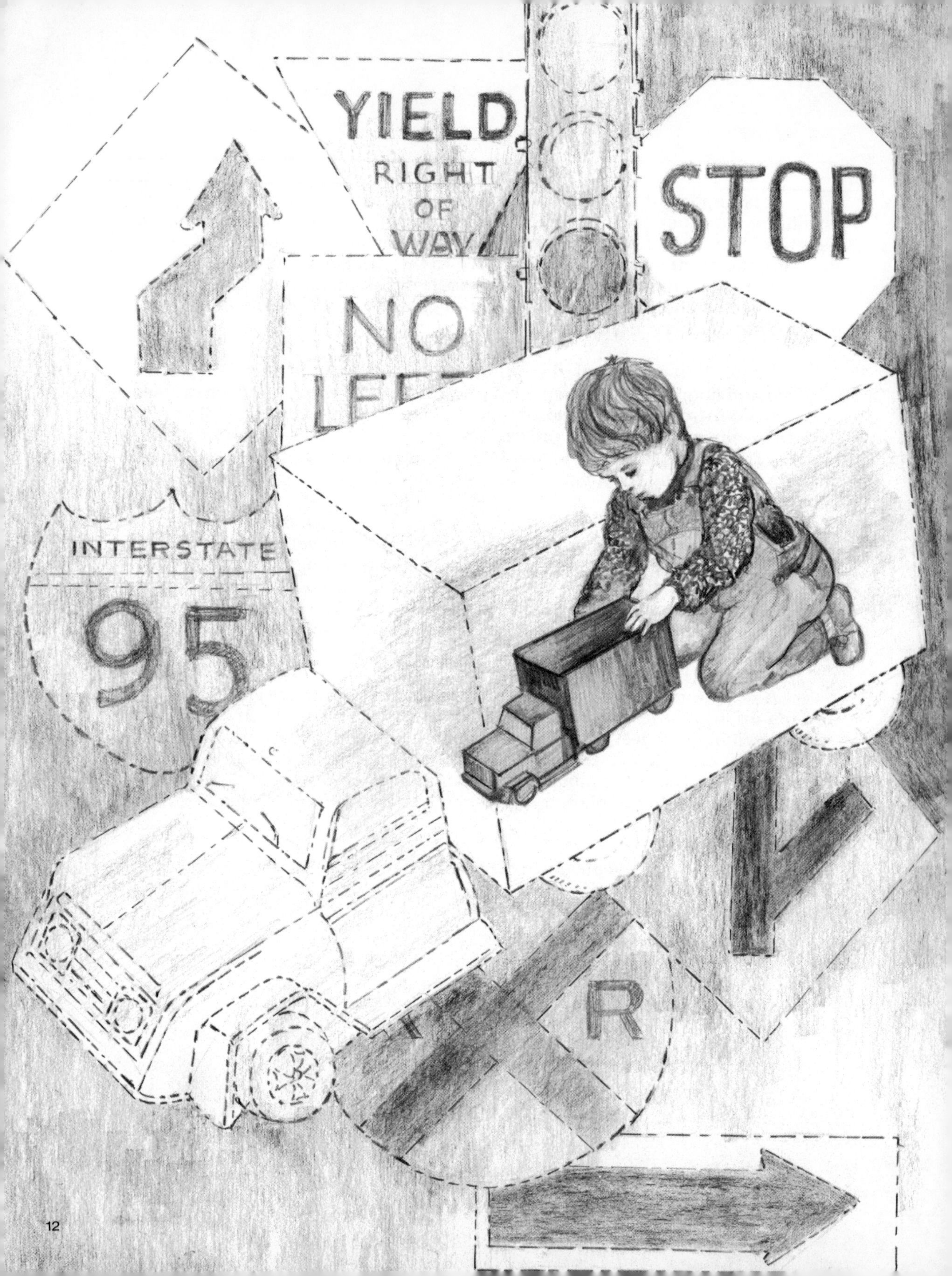
YIELD
RIGHT
OF
WAY
STOP
NO
INTERSTATE
95
R

Introduction

3 YEAR OLDS

An infant is busy establishing himself as a separate entity, a being apart from his mother. A two-year-old incorporates *me, mine,* and *no* into his vocabulary as the beginning step in finding out who he is. By the time the child reaches three, he is ready to embark on a more extensive exploration of himself and his world.

Have you ever watched a three-year-old be a truck? He is on his hands and knees, utterly absorbed in pushing a truck, some other object, or himself across the floor, zooming around curves and accompanying himself with appropriate guttural sounds. He *is* the truck, and he wants to be all the things he encounters. He is constantly exploring what it is like to be mother, father, a dog, a rabbit, a car.

He also needs games that allow his imagination to soar and allow him to express his feelings. He is just beginning to sense that he can expect some things from himself and some things from others. This leads him to play some very rudimentary group games, especially those in which he can skip, gallop, hop, and jump.

Dress Up

Players: One or more children

Materials: A mirror, an old suitcase or a box with an assortment of old hats, scarves, skirts, high-heeled shoes, capes, boots, ties, hats, and so on.

The Game: The child puts on what he wants in accordance with who he wants to be that day.

Comment: The child is curious about the mysterious ways in which all creatures function. Role playing is the child's attempt to recognize, understand, and incorporate others by being them. This is the way he understands who he is, who you are, and why. More importantly, it's a move toward the development of empathy.

This quest is based in reality but almost always mixed with fantasy. Dealing with reality demands empirical knowledge, something the child of three hasn't had time enough to acquire, so he inevitably uses fantasy. A mirror is essential to Dress Up because the child likes to see what he looks like and what he acts like.

Dress Up is an essential game because role playing never really stops; nor does the search for role models. The question "Who am I?" is never satisfactorily answered (perhaps fortunately).

Dialogues

Players: One adult, one child

The Game: In this game the adult poses questions that lead the child to think about the world around him. The range of questions has no limit. One topic can lead to a long discussion on that subject or the subject can keep switching. For instance:

    Q. How do you think a fish feels, living in water all day and all night?

    Q. How do you think snakes like being snakes since most can't do anything but crawl?

    Q. If you had to be a machine of any kind, what would you be?

    Q. Do you think those zebras we saw at the zoo mind being so far away from the place where they were born and so far away from their families?

(If this brings forth an answer about how terrible it is to be away from Mommy or Daddy, the parent may be on his way to discovering what happened that day that distressed the child.)

Answers to questions are sometimes unexpected:

    Q. If you could talk to a tree, what questions would you ask it?
    A. Would you like to come into the house? *Or*
    A. Don't your arms hurt? *Or*
    A. What do you do when you have an itch?

A most interesting question is: If you were an animal, what animal would you be?

Answers range from: I would be a *Tyrannosaurus rex* and I would be King of the World. I would be a tiger and chew everyone up and I would live in a dark, ugly place. I would be an eagle and I would fly over everyone and I would see everything. I would be a dog and have a nice home and be taken care of. I would be a pet in a nursery school and all the children would play with me.

More often than not, the answer to this question involves strong animals—snakes, dinosaurs, alligators, and big birds.

Comment: Dialogues between parent and child are an important part of their relationship. This game is specifically designed to help the parent encourage the child's exploration of the world around him. The answers give the child an opportunity to express his feelings—even the most dark and angry feelings—in an acceptable way. He has learned he is not allowed to chew everyone up, fight, punch, or bite, and he needs an outlet for aggression and frustration. (A child in a less aggressive mood may indicate that by saying he'd like to be a domestic pet.)

If the child seems sad or hurt, these dialogues may be able to help reveal the source of the trouble in a less embarrassing, more spontaneous way than a direct question about why the child is feeling bad.

The most common fantasies are of flying and power. The all-seeing power of the eagle is frequently expressed. It's a reaction to being small and keenly aware of being surrounded by people who are bigger and know more. He who sees more knows more and has a better command over his world.

The Turtle Race

Players: One adult (narrator), one or more children

The Game: The narrator tells the following story:

Once upon a time, there was a turtle who decided he would go into a race. So the race began and the turtle started to run and he was running very slowly and he was very happy and a horse ran by. And he was galloping. [Narrator runs in place to imitate galloping sound, and children follow suit.] And the horse ran by and the turtle kept running and running and he was going his own very slow way and the turtle kept trying and a dog ran by [Narrator and children stamp lightly on floor to indicate dog] and the turtle was struggling and struggling and he kept saying, "I'm going to make it to the finish, I'm going to make it to the finish," and a bird flew by [Narrator and children make whooshing sound] and the turtle is still going and going and a rabbit hops by [Narrator and children make hopping sound] and the turtle is still trying and he's still going and he keeps saying, "I'm going to make it to the finish," and an elephant steps by and he almost steps on the turtle and the elephant lumbers past the turtle and the turtle keeps going and going and he says, "I'm going to make it to the finish," and finally the turtle sees the finish line and he says, "I'm going to make it, I'm going to make it," and—finally he comes to the finish line and he finishes the race.

Immediately and inevitably all the children cry, "Did he win?" Narrator: "Yes, he did. He did win because he did what he set out to do. He finished the race."

Comment: The obvious lesson is that the turtle won the race because he accomplished his goal. If you can teach the child it doesn't matter if he gets there first or not, that child will be spared a lot of pressure. Everybody's ultimate goal is to do activities well, something that can only be accomplished if all the building blocks required to develop skills properly are in place and have been put there in accordance with one's own particular timing.

A child who is pushed may lose confidence because if he is pressured into going too fast, the pieces that must be assembled to achieve true skill are often skipped. Taking the time to build a solid foundation is crucial. By being too eager to "win," one runs the risk of weakening the foundation. This applies cogently, for example, to basic learning skills such as reading and writing. The most effective way to learn these skills is to develop a solid foundation based on the child's individual pattern of maturation. In this game there is no advantage in being first; it is also true that the child who learns to read first is by no means certain to end up reading best.

The turtle story is a much-loved one. It or a parent's variation on the theme can be repeated ad infinitum. One can never tire of hearing that a loser can be a winner!

Closets

also known as Under the Table, Bed, or Chair, etc.

Players: One or more children

The Game: For reasons we cannot explain, this game comes naturally to children, beginning around age three. One, two, or three children get into a closet or other cramped quarters and stay there, sometimes for a very long time. As far as older eyes and ears can make out, they are doing nothing. This activity makes some parents very nervous and all parents curious.

Comment: We don't know what children who play this game are doing, or why. Perhaps it's based on a need for a time away from parents and everyday pressures or on a desire for separateness. Keeping it secret may give the child a rare opportunity to experience power. And maybe, if you tax your memory, you can remember what you did in the closet.

Sort-It-Out

Players: One adult, one or more children

The Game: The child is challenged to sort household objects according to different classifications. The younger child will sort for color, size, or shape, perhaps by putting colored buttons into egg cartons. The older child will be able to take on more complicated sorting tasks, such as separating items according to "what you clean with, what you cook with, and what you eat with" (i.e., sorting flatware into separate piles). Putting pennies, dimes, nickels, and quarters into different containers is a game particularly enjoyed by the older child.

How Is a Cat Like a Dog/ How Are They Different?

Players: One or more children

The Game: The child is asked to compare and contrast, in as many ways as he can, two somewhat similar things. The observant three-year-old should be encouraged to say more in answer to the question than that they are both animals; that a dog barks and a cat meows. He can point out that they both have four legs, tails, fur, generally don't bite, don't like each other, etc. He is likely to know that dogs are usually bigger, that cats are more likely to scratch, and also purr. The child should be urged to think of as many specifics as he possibly can.

Comment: Classification, as in the preceding two games, is a skill that must be mastered, since virtually all knowledge is classified. How is a car like a boat/how are they different—a house like an apartment—a river like a sea—a hill like a mountain? The ability to classify is an invaluable aid in improving the child's knowledge of the world and increasing his powers of observation. In French nursery schools this game is called, *Vive la différence.*

Clap Syllables

Players: One adult, one or more children

The Game: A child learns to break down words into their syllabic pieces by clapping with each complete sound. In the beginning the adult claps each time he pronounces a syllable of any word: rab/bit, sa/la/mi; gal/lop; hip/po/pot/a/mus. As the child learns to break down words, he picks his own word and syllabifies it with claps.

HIP/PO/POT/A/MUS

Beginning Sounds

Players: One adult, one or more children

The Game: The adult chooses beginning sounds of words and groups them. The *s* sound is a top favorite and a good one with which to start. Ask the child to say any words that begin with an s-s-s-s: snakes, slices, slide. Or any words that begin with the sound r-r-r-r: rabbit, rust, wriggle, red. For fun, encourage the child to exaggerate the beginning sound.

Rhyming

Players: One adult, one or more children

The Game: The adult asks what words the child can think of that belong in the *at* family. The child may need a little help getting started. The adult can suggest cat, rat, bat, or sat. Then the adult may move to words in the *it* family: sit, hit, bit, and lit.

Comment: These games help develop language and reading skills by showing how words are made up of smaller building blocks and how the sounds and symbols often occur in common groups or families. All auditory language skills are helpful later when the child must learn to connect auditory to visual language skills. Meanwhile, his ability to communicate improves.

Playing these games with a three-year-old is a useful way to help prepare him to learn to read.

Flannel Board Games

Note: The flannel board is an excellent and ongoing learning device, useful both at home and at school. It's simple to make and can be used for a variety of games for children from three through five.

Materials: A piece of cardboard, lap size or larger. A piece of dark-colored (navy, gray, black) wool, flannel, or felt, cut one-and-a-half inches larger on all four sides than the cardboard. Masking tape to attach material to back of board. A yard or two or more of felt in a contrasting bright color. Soft lead pencil for tracing letters, numbers, characters, and shapes onto brightly colored felt. Scissors to cut out same. Felt pieces will stick to wool, flannel, or felt and pull off easily. The board is used for a variety of games including:

Pick-a-Letter

Players: One adult, one or more children

The Game: The adult traces and then cuts out (of wool, flannel, or felt) the capital letters of the alphabet. It is important to make all letters capital and big in size. First the adult asks the child to pick a letter at random and put it on the board. Then he tells the child the name of the letter. After the child has learned to recognize letters, the adult can ask if he can pick out a *C* or a *P* or an *M* from the pile and put it on the board. Much later on, the child is challenged to match small and capital letters and to pick letters to spell beginning words.

Find-a-Number

Players: One adult, one or more children

The Game: This is played the same way as Pick-a-Letter. Later on, after the child can recognize the numbers from one to ten, he can learn to put them in consecutive order.

Comment: A child begins learning to discriminate among different symbols by first becoming familiar with basic shapes such as circles, squares, triangles, oblongs, etc.

Learning shapes and symbols is fundamental in the acquisition of language and should be "built into" the child by all means available. Tracing letters with a pencil, tracing a flannel shape with the finger, or forming symbols with the finger in sand or snow uses tactile and kinesthetic impressions to "imprint" the learning. Repetition of these various "exercises" helps to build in the learning. The greater the variety of ways in which a symbol can be experienced, the more effectively it is incorporated and the more fully is its signification absorbed.

These games, always played for fun, present a quick and easy way for the child to learn to recognize the symbols that form the alphabet and to differentiate between the shape of a 2 and a 3.

Story Board

Players: One adult, one or more children

The Game: The adult enhances the narration of familiar stories such as "Little Red Riding Hood," "Jack and the Beanstalk," "The Three Bears," etc., by the use of flannel board props. If "The Three Bears" is chosen, trace the bears, the bowls, the beds, the chairs, and the table onto the wool, flannel, or felt from pictures in a book and cut them out. Tell the child the story, sticking on the props as you go.

Holiday Board

Players: One adult, one or more children

The Game: This is a version of the game above that can use as much imagination as a parent wants to put into it. The adult builds a story around, for instance, the Pilgrims and the Indians at Thanksgiving; Santa Claus at Christmas; the witch on her broomstick at Halloween; or the Easter Bunny. Simple stick figures can be cut out freehand or even during the narration of the story to put on the board.

Comment: Action (putting figures onto the board) plus narration makes story-telling much more exciting. The adult can start this game by taking the initiative, but as the game progresses and if the child seems eager to be more active, the adult can assume an increasingly passive role. Eventually, the child takes great pleasure in placing the figures on the board himself and in telling the story to anybody he can inveigle into listening.

What's Missing?

Players: One adult, one child

The Game: Put an assortment of objects, such as a feather, a sock, a penny, or a banana, on a tray and show it to the child. (Objects can be limitless in variety—paper clips, cookies, a piece of cotton, an ashtray, a thimble, a pencil holder, a bottle of glue, a fork, and on and on.) Ask the child to close his eyes. Take something away, tell the child to look again, and ask him to identify the missing object.

The older he is, the greater the number of objects can be. A very young child could start with just two or three objects.

Comment: This game exercises powers of observation and short-term memory span. The child experiences great excitement as he studies the objects before him, as he *knows* there will be an unknown. The next time he looks, *something will be missing*!!

Amazing Mazes

Players: One child

Materials: Paper and pencil

The Game: The child must find his way through increasingly obstructed paths. Simple mazes follow a path beginning with no pitfalls. The next stage involves a maze with only one trick, which the child conquers by trial and error. As the child gets older, mazes of increasing complexity are used. See samples.

Comment: Mazes are an important teaching tool because they require judgment and abstract reasoning ability. As the child grows he develops the ability to look ahead and visualize—he looks at the maze and processes it mentally before doing the operation. This is an exercise in thinking through an operation before actually performing it.

Bowl Holders

Players: One or more children

Materials: Graduated or different-sized cardboard or plastic containers or bowls. Empty plastic shampoo or liquid soap bottles.

The Game: The object is to fit one container inside another. These same containers are also used in water play, during which water is poured from one to another.

Comment: The variety of containers and things that can be put into them is limitless, just as "in and out" is endlessly intriguing and has many philosophic implications. "In and out" is a species of the genus "doing and undoing," the process that (falsely) reassures us that nothing need be irrevocable and so gives us the courage to keep trying.

Direction Word Play

Players: One adult, one child

Materials: String or masking tape, table, objects

The Game: Divide the table in half by placing string or masking tape across the center. Put two distinct objects, such as a small basket and a jar lid, on each side. Give the child a third object, such as a crayon, and tell him to:

Put the crayon under the basket (or lid)
Put the crayon on top of the basket (or lid)
Put the crayon in between the basket and lid
Put the crayon over the lid
Put the crayon in the basket
Put the crayon as close to the lid as possible
Put the crayon as far away from the basket as possible

Put the crayon into the basket (or lid)
Put the crayon into the lid, and put them both beside the basket
Put the crayon opposite to the lid

Comment: This game and Bowl Holders help the child master spatial relationships. Certain words serve the essentially geographic function of orienting us and objects in space. This is necessary for establishing the location of the physical self in relation to other physical objects and for locating objects with reference to each other. "Knowing where it's at" is an endlessly useful skill, for as time goes on and we gain access to more and more space, we do need objects for orientation.

True or False?

Players: One adult, one or more children

The Game: Make a statement and ask the child to say whether it is true or false. Be sure to adapt the sophistication of the statement to the child's age. Often the more preposterous the statement, the more spirited the game.

Comment: The purpose is to increase familiarity with words and facts. The added element is the sense of mastery and the pleasure the child gets out of recognizing the absurd in statements such as, "Cows come in purple and green," or, to an older child, "Monkeys fly." The child's greatest pleasure comes when he thinks up the absurdities himself: snakes hop, birds bark, snow is blue, rain is dry.

Animal Travel

Note: At three, the child understands start and finish and can gallop, walk, trot, and sometimes even skip.

Players: One adult, one or more children

The Game: Children take great pleasure in identifying and imitating the movements of animals. When asked what the toad does, the child will answer, "He hops," and begin to hop. The adults can then ask the same question about every conceivable animal. With enthusiasm the child is a horse galloping, a turtle crawling, a bird flying, or a lion stalking. Children will imitate all these gaits at any time, no matter where they are. In getting to the table, the door, the elevator, or their beds, they will often employ an animal gait.

Comment: The child's fascination with animal gaits equals his love of movement. Galloping, walking, trotting and crawling feel freeing and satisfying to the child. Gaits develop large-muscle skills and in this game the parent teaches his child a bit of animal lore at the same time. As the child's horizons expand, the parent can zero in on more esoteric animals. What does the gnu do? The wallaby? The sloth? As soon as the question is asked the child goes into his version of how that animal travels.

This game takes on an added dimension when done to music. Music is played in different rhythms and the child is asked to move in time to the music. Almost every child is excited by sudden changes of tempo. The child can also be asked which animal the music represents—this is a basic and lovely exercise in musical interpretation.

Sammy

Players: One adult, one or more children

The Game: Here's another chance to imitate animals. The following verses, with or without music, seem universally popular:

This is the story about Sammy.
His father sent him out to buy bread,
But Sammy didn't feel like walking.
He wished he could [choose a movement such as crawl, fly, hop, jump, run, gallop, etc.] instead.
And he said:
If I were a [animal that fits movement] I would [movement] to the store,
[Movement] to the store, [movement] to the store.
If I were a [animal] I would [movement] to the store,
For my father.

For example:

If I were a horse I would gallop to the store,
Gallop to the store, gallop to the store.
If I were a horse I would gallop to the store,
For my father.

Repeat the first verse and substitute a different animal and movement in the second verse. Then add final verses:

Now, Sammy remembered about the loaf of bread
And thought he'd better get along,
And as he started walking
He made up a brand new song.
And he said:
I'm glad I'm *me* and I'm walking to the store,
Walking to the store, walking to the store.
I'm glad I'm *me* and I'm walking to the store,
For my father.

Comment: This game gives the child a chance to use his imagination and to exercise his large muscles by mastering these gaits. Its greatest significance, however, is that it focuses attention on the self as "that which experiences." The child turns himself into whatever animal he likes, and then returns to who *he* is once again!

Warm Up

Players: One adult, one child

The Game: The adult does formal or informal warm-up exercises with the child. Stretching, running, and twisting movements done at a slow and then quicker pace may be incorporated; however, the adult should be careful to see that he is not pushing the child past his limits.

Comment: This is immediately identified in the child's mind as a grown-up ritual and gives him a fine sense of gratification. It makes a child feel important to be genuinely included in serious adult activities. He also feels a tremendous joy in mastering his body.

Brass Wagon

Players: One adult, four or more children

The Game: Everybody stands in a circle holding hands. While getting into position, the parent asks the children to listen closely and starts singing the first verse (see music):

> Let's tap feet, the old brass wa-gon.
> Let's tap feet, the old brass wa-gon.
> Let's tap feet, the old brass wa-gon.
> We'll all tap feet to-day.

Inevitably, the children start tapping before the end of the verse is reached. At that point, the parent says "Next," and launches into the song again using any of the suggestions below:

> Tap your feet
> Circle to the right/left
> Nod your head
> Clap your hands
> Jump up and down
> Make a funny face
> Turn all around
> Sit right down

Comment: This gait game is multifaceted because it combines intimacy (holding hands and performing different actions in unison with others) with control of body movements, following directions, maintaining rhythm, and the coordination of all of the above. Most respond enthusiastically to music combined with movement. Any game incorporating both relieves tension and encourages a positive atmosphere.

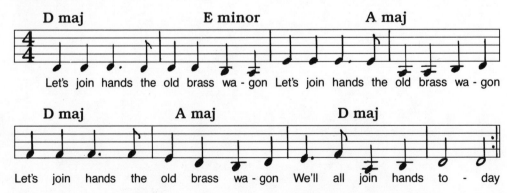

40

Balloon Ball

Players: One adult, six or more children

The Game: Divide the players into teams of three or four each. Give each group a different-colored balloon. The groups can name themselves according to the color of their balloon—the pink crowd, the yellow crowd, etc. Explain that the object is for each team to keep their balloon in the air and moving; the team who lets the balloon fall on the floor or get out of control loses.

Comment: This game represents a beginning experience with competition in that the teams, not the individuals, are the winners or losers. It's a start toward preparing children for the possibility that they might sometimes lose.

Sardines

Players: One adult, four or more children

The Game: Darken the house. The child chosen to be "It" is given three minutes to hide and, with the help of an adult who knows the house, finds a closet or cupboard to hide in. The rest of the children go off to look for him and, as each child finds him or her, they too squeeze into the same hiding place. After a short while the tiny space is usually filled with gleeful giggles and squished little bodies!

Comment: Three-year-olds enjoy physical contact which, in this game, is the reward for finding and joining the independent player.

The eternal favorite upon which this is based, Hide and Seek, is the most appealing game of all because it's related to the child's continued need to work through the separation process. Hide and Seek is his method of assuring himself that he can survive on his own, however briefly, and he is able to reassure himself that contact can be reestablished. Separation and reunion, tension and resolution are important cycles in the life process.

Musical Chairs

Players: One adult, eight or more children

The Game: Line up eight chairs (or more—the same number of chairs as there are children) in a row with every other chair facing the opposite direction. Ask the children to sit down quietly and listen closely to the music you are about to play. Explain that the minute the music begins, they are to get up and start walking, not running, around the chairs. When the music stops they must sit down as fast as they can.

Comment: This game is harder to play than one thinks and usually brings on an attack of the giggles when a child attempts to sit down too fast and misses the chair. It is a deliberately noncompetitive version of Musical Chairs, because a three-year-old is too young to cope with the isolation of being "out." This version gives the child a sense of group play while at the same time keeping him in suspense as he waits for the music to stop and start.

Statues

Players: One adult, six or more children

The Game: Everyone but "It" gets into positions of their choice. "It" tries to make any one of the other players laugh or move, and the first one who laughs or moves becomes "It."

Comment: Statues involves changing roles (from "It" to a statue and back) and physical and social tension. This game challenges the child's ability to control his body and his emotions. Most children are on the brink of laughter as they struggle to keep from moving no matter what "It" does. They sense that "control" is of the essence, and the tension involved is thrilling!

Bluebird

Players: One adult, four or more children

The Game: Have the children form a circle. Ask one child to stand in the center. Explain that the children in the circle will walk around holding hands, while chanting: "Bluebird, Bluebird, in and out my window." As "window" is said, the children all raise their arms to let "Bluebird" (the child in the center) out of the "window." They bring their arms down as soon as Bluebird is outside the circle, continue walking around and immediately begin their chant again. During the second chant, the children raise their arms again on "window," and Bluebird reenters the circle. This is repeated until Bluebird has gone in and out of every "window." Then another child takes on the role of Bluebird.

Comment: Even though teams as such are not involved, Bluebird is a good beginning game for team play because it's simple, it calls for group action, and the child who is Bluebird is never alone. The other children are actually helping him as they allow the child "in" and "out."

Introduction

Here comes the conquering hero—with a problem. More often than not he is brash, negative, and loud. Pity the four-year-old, for he is at a vulnerable age and suffering from a heightened perception of his own sense of helplessness. At four, the child acts out being a superhero or a terrible monster, perhaps because he hopes through his imagination to overcome a potentially overwhelming powerlessness.

To a great extent, he has accomplished the goals of the three-year-old. He has managed to get a line on the other guy and he sees his peers as people he can cooperate with rather than simply as threats. Other people are seen as part of his world partly because he is beginning to learn what their expectations of him are and what he can expect of them. He has learned limits; as aggressive as he may be, he somewhat restrains a tendency to grab, hit, or bite, not because he wants to be good but because it doesn't always pay.

Mastery and power are the key words for a four-year-old. Any game he plays is to enhance his sense of safety, self, and bigness.

Dress Up

Players: One or more children

Materials: A mirror. A trunk or box with old clothes plus accessories.

The Game: Dress Up is very important to the four-year-old. It gives him a chance to act out his aggressions and the temporary illusion of power when he puts on a cape and "flies" around the room as Superman. At three, he would put on almost anything indiscriminately; at four, he puts on something blue to act out the role of a police officer for which he requires "equipment"—badge, walkie-talkie, cap, police car, whistle, billy club, etc. He may dress up as an astronaut to man a space shuttle or act as the ringmaster in the lion or elephant ring. A piece of aluminum foil will serve as a badge, an egg crate can be a space shuttle, and a piece of string might be a ringmaster's whip.

Comment: By the roles he chooses the child reveals himself to you. Subtlety is not an outstanding trait at this age. Under the "protection" of someone else's role, he will allow many of his thoughts, fears, and desires to emerge.

On with the Story!

Players: One adult, one or more children

The Game: This is an extension of the dialogue game and can be done with children of any age. The parent starts making up a story and the child either finishes it, or continues it by taking turns with the parent who adds sentences. The very young child appreciates stories set around familiar, domestic scenes, such as going to the supermarket. The three-year-old likes stories about trips to the zoo or the forest or the seashore and the four-year-old to five-year-old likes stories that involve more adventurous explorations.

For a four-year-old, try beginnings like these: Once there was a space ship that went flying off into the atmosphere and it bumped into a talking star, *or* once upon a time there was a big storm and there were some animals roaming around who were very confused, *or* once upon a time some children were talking in the forest and they came upon a cave. Inside the cave there was a _____.

Comment: This game employs memory and recall in the younger child and exercises imagination in one who is older. It is very useful for a four- or five-year-old child who is both fascinated and frightened by scary creatures. He may express those fears in a story set in the forest, on the sea, in the mountains, or in a dark house, and will often come up with some species of frightening beast who lurks in one of these places. The beast may represent any threat the child experiences in life and, as author of the story, in overcoming the beast he attempts to conquer the fear.

That's My Voice

Players: One or more children

The Game: Tape recorders hold universal appeal and the child who has learned to operate one by himself can give free reign to his imagination. After a child is taught how to use one, he will probably spend many happy hours making up stories alone or with a friend and playing them back again and again. The four-year-old is just beginning to think about making up plays and stage dramas crammed, no doubt, with jungle beasts, monsters, and astronauts.

Comment: Listening to his own voice fascinates the four-year-old because it represents the self he is trying so hard to grasp. "Listen, it's me! It's me!" The reproduction of his voice is objective evidence that his self is real and has the power to be heard, without a doubt, by others. The yearning for that power is the reason four-year-olds tend to be so loud.

What Hurts?

Players: Two or more children

Materials: Box of bandages, tongue depressors, blunt scissors, stethoscope, ear syringe, wooden tongs, toy injection needle. (The more props the parent can provide, the better.) Patients can be a doll, a friend, the child himself, a stuffed animal, Mommy, etc.

The Game: The child plays he is the doctor or nurse equipped with all of the "necessary" instruments. When he is with a friend, the child may occasionally elect to play the part of the patient. The "examination" can take place anywhere and props are best kept in a doctor/nurse box (perhaps decorated in red and white!).

Comment: Familiarity overcomes fear. Playing the role of doctor or nurse is the way a child puts himself in a danger-free position. It makes the doctor's use of instruments less menacing to the child. Again, his imagination comes to his aid, changing him from the helpless individual at the mercy of the other to the person in control, the one with the power. Perhaps the major attraction of this game is based less on fear of the doctor than an attraction to his magical power to make things better.

The Geo Board

Players: One or more children

Materials: A piece of smooth wood twelve inches by twelve inches and about one inch thick. One-and-a-half-inch screws placed one-and-a-half inches apart. Screws must always be equidistantly placed (the older the child, the less space between the screws). A box of different-colored, different-sized rubber bands to place on the screws. Geo boards, which are relatively easy to make, can also be bought in school-supply stores.

The Game: The child puts rubber bands (see illustration) around the screws in an unlimited number of combinations. He can create shapes within shapes, divide up shapes, make oblongs, squares, triangles, hexagons, or any shape that is angular and varicolored. This game is often played by two, sometimes three children. One child will make up a design and challenge his friend to duplicate it.

Comment: The geo board is a recommended teaching tool for this age and provides a good opportunity for parental participation. It's fun; it involves spatial perception, eye-hand coordination, and creativity in making up designs, and it gives the child a sense of mastery. It also provides a basic introduction to geometric concepts and, last but hardly least, it taps the child's game-playing skill when he challenges a friend or a parent.

Flannel Board Games

Note: See page 26 for construction.

Beginning Letters

Players: One adult, one or more children

The Game: Show the child a picture of, for instance, a cat or a hat; put the last two letters of the word on the board (*AT* in this case) and see if the child can find the beginning letter of the word, sometimes referred to as the beginning sound letter. Objects should be grouped by word families, i.e., the *AT* family, the *IT* family, etc.

How Many?

Players: One adult, one or more children

Materials (in addition to flannel board): Ten small objects such as raisins, paper clips, or toy cars.

The Game: Offer the child one or more objects. Ask him to put the number that "tells" how many objects he has on the board.

Comment: These games offer practice in symbol formation and the opportunity to learn how symbols are used. They also relate visual to verbal symbols. In the first game, for instance, there is no actual "object" directly involved. A cat, however, may be represented by a picture, by the written word the child forms, or by the spoken word he sounds out. In the second game, on the other hand, the objects are right there demonstrating their number and challenging the child to select the correct symbol to represent that number.

Story Board

Players: One adult, one or more children

The Game: The parent cuts out of the flannel rudimentary stick figures or objects to make up stories that interest the child. The range of cutouts can include dolls; animals; humans; circles for planets, vehicles, and airplanes; squares for houses and schools and so on. The child is urged to make up a story about any objects he chooses to put on the board.

Comment: While at four the child still craves storytelling or reading-aloud sessions with his parents, he wants to and should be encouraged to lead. The four-year-old version of the flannel board Story Game is designed to aid the development of expressive language and help the child learn the art of narration through bringing order to his thoughts and connecting chains of events.

Object Alphabet Game

Players: One adult, one or more children

Materials: Small objects found around the house, such as notebooks, kites, boxes, toy cars or trucks, pens, books, and so on. Index cards with, for four-year-olds, one *capital* letter of the alphabet on each. Lower-case letters may be used for five-year-olds.

The Game: The objects are placed on a table in front of the child who then hunts for a letter in the stack that has the same beginning sound as the selected object.

Note: Adults should be careful not to select objects that, for the beginner, are spelled in a confusing way. Words like *photograph* and *thimble* may, if offered too soon, stand in the way of a child's ability to grasp the connection between certain letters and sounds.

Comment: This game teaches letter recognition along with the understanding that the symbols (letters) represent sound. Involving the child in the act of symbol recognition (saying the sound and selecting the letter) makes the experience real and gives it personal meaning.

Switch!

Players: One adult, one or more children

Materials: Any living-room, kitchen, or child's-room objects such as boxes, pencil sharpeners, eating utensils, coasters, soup cans, toys, playing cards, photographs, small statues, etc.

The Game: The parent lines up four or five objects on a table or on the floor. The child is asked to look at the objects and memorize their positions. Then he is asked to close his eyes for ten seconds (no peeking) while the parent switches them around. The child puts them back in their original order. Parent and child take turns.

Comment: This game is tremendously stimulating to the child's powers of observation and exercises short-term memory span. Most children enjoy becoming skillful at this game as they see themselves mastering increasingly challenging object assortments. This is especially true as the items become less disparate. *You* try memorizing a lineup of objects that include two statues facing left; two bunnies, one with the left ear flopping, the other with the right flopping; and three cans of Campbell's soup, one tomato, one pea, one chicken. Naturally, all get switched. Children enjoy this game and at the Nursery ask to play it every day.

One Hairy Hen

Players: One adult, two or more children

The Game: Have the children sit in a row. The first child says, "One hairy hen"; the second says, "One hairy hen, two daffy ducks." Each player adds an animal plus a description and must repeat all that has gone before. Any one-word description the child thinks of is acceptable. Possible order could be: three giggling geese; four red robins; five pretty pigeons; six crazy cranes; seven pale parrots; eight old owls; nine big buzzards; ten eager eagles. The adjective does not have to start with the same letter as the animal.

Comment: This game sharpens short-term auditory recall, makes the imagination go to work, and enriches both knowledge and vocabulary.

Cleaned, Cooked, Boiled Rat Bones

Players: One or more children

Materials: Water in any large container (sink, bathtub, baby bath, wading pool, water table). Playthings include plastic tubes, funnels, strainers, empty dishwashing-liquid containers, pots, pans, measuring spoons, sponges, etc.

The Game: Provide the child or children with the above and watch them as they concoct all kinds of "mixtures." (Note: It's never safe to leave young children alone even for seconds with water at hand.) The more containers there are, the more complicated the formula for each potion becomes!

Comment: Four-year-olds often use water play as a springboard for fantasy. We recently watched a group of four-year-olds as they prepared a potion made of "cleaned, cooked, boiled rat bones from rats raised on mosquito soup." The potion was an "experiment" to see if it could be used on "bad guys." (It was not to turn them into "good guys.")

Water play is fun for most young children and is in itself soothing. Play with water offers the child the opportunity to experiment with measurement, volume, floating and sinking, and density, and is used at each stage of growth in ways appropriate to developmental issues. Younger children can trace shapes in water with a finger or hand, much as they might do in sand or snow. The shape will not remain but the muscle patterning, if repeated often enough, will.

Lotto Alphabet Game

Players: One adult, one or more children

Materials: Eight-and-one-half-by-eleven-inch plain paper, pencil, ruler, and scissors to cut up index cards. Make two lotto boards by ruling one piece of paper into sixteen two-inch squares, the other into nine two-inch squares, with the center box divided horizontally in two. (See below.) Cut index cards into approximate two-inch squares, write each letter of the alphabet onto twenty-five squares, and print the *O* and *X* together on the twenty-sixth index card before cutting it in half. Write the letters of the alphabet on each square of the lotto boards—*O* and *X* will each end up being two rectangles. Use only capital letters for the younger child.

The Game: The object is for the child to match the cards with the letters on the lotto board. (When he is older, use capital letters on the lotto board and small letters on the cards and ask the child to match them up.)

Lotto Color Game

Players: One adult, one or more children

Materials: In addition to those mentioned in the Lotto Alphabet Game, colored crayons or paints are needed. Make one lotto board by ruling one piece of paper into nine two-inch squares. Color individual squares red, green, black, white, brown, blue, yellow, orange, and purple. Cut index cards into approximate two-inch squares and write out (in capitals) each color on the squares in the color it represents.

The Game: Ask the child to match the cards to the lotto board. Later, as the child's reading ability increases, write the colors in black.

Comment: These matching games involve recognition and meaning, perception and interpretation. At first, these skills are primitive and involve only "same" and "different." With increasing maturity "same" can be graded into "identical" and "similar" and "different" can be qualified as well. As the art of perception increases, one learns quantitative and qualitative distinctions, and is able to group accordingly.

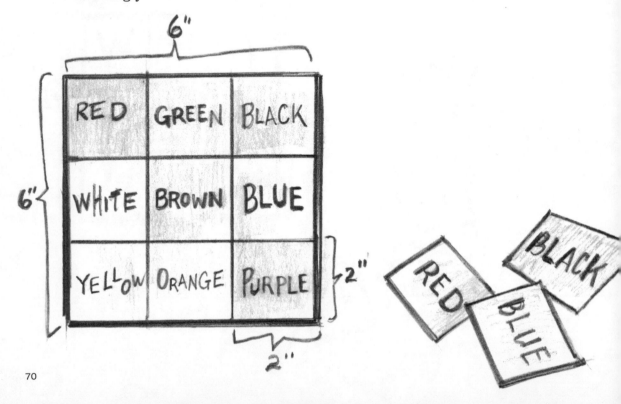

Run and Stop

Players: One adult, one or more children

The Game: The child and/or adult can choose the movement. (See verse below.) The adult sings or chants the following verse and instructs the child to freeze at the word "*stop*." Then the verse is repeated. Any tune or chant is acceptable.

> Oh, you run [or jump, hop, skate, fly, twirl, roll, etc.] and you run and you *stop*,
> And you run and you run and you *stop*,
> [Faster] And you run and you run and
> You run and you *stop*.

Comment: In addition to the large-muscle development involved, control is needed to play this game. It's not so easy to start and stop, start and stop. Children love this game because it challenges them and tension-release is involved. Tension is built up as they wait for the anticipated *stop* and released when the command is given.

The Way We Go!

Players: One adult, one or more children

The Game: The parent thinks up various gaits (walk, jump, hop, skip, run, skate) and/or varied steps (walk three steps forward, take one back; walk two steps forward, take one to the right, then one to the left) for the child to perform en route to school, market, and/or any other place. Here the parent is asked to call on his imagination, since this game can be varied in any number of ways by the use of simple chants or tunes and by changing directions. For instance, the parent can sing or chant:

> This is the way we walk to school,
> Walk to school,
> Walk to school.
> Take three steps forward, then one back.
> [Repeat]
> [Repeat]
> Now we take one step to the left
> And one to the right
> And three steps forward and we stop
> And do it again.
> One step to the left
> And one to the right
> And three steps forward and we stop
> And this time
> We trot like a horse,
> Trot like a horse,
> Trot like a horse.

Comment: All gait games are designed to enhance the child's large-muscle skills in ways that are fun. This game combines muscle control and concentration in a spirited and playful way. The child is challenged to understand and react to the imaginative command as quickly as he can.

Simon Says Move

Players: One adult, one or more children

The Game: This gait game emphasizes the recognition that every consonant in the alphabet is a beginning word sound; i.e., the sound *buh* fits ball, boy, bat; the sound *s-s-s* fits snake, sat, some; the sound *th* fits three, think, thin, and so on.

Tell the child that in this version of "Simon Says" the child is to do one of the movements listed below when Simon says a word that has a certain beginning sound. For instance, when Simon says a word beginning with *m-m-m*, the child should hop. Then start by saying three or four words that do not begin with *m-m-m*, such as piano, cake and rug, pausing after each word and finally ending up with the word "monkey." Immediately the child will hop (if he's listening carefully!).

Examples: "Simon says *tap* when you hear the beginning sound *d-d-d*; now; come; me; dog." (On hearing "dog," the child starts tapping.)

"Simon says *wiggle* when you hear the beginning sound *g-g-g*; sky; Alice; get." (On hearing "get," the child wiggles.)

"Simon says *flap* when you hear the beginning sound *n-n-n*; some; moon; tree; full; not." (On hearing "not," the child flaps his arms.)

The variety of motions Simon can think up is probably endless. Here are some we have used in the Nursery: shake, clap, tap, jump, hop, bend, bow, twist, wave, sway, flap, nod, blink, chatter, wiggle, turn around, sit, blow, stretch, freeze.

Comment: This is an ingenious game that combines the child's pleasure in spirited movements with the development of language skills. The child must concentrate on listening intently as he waits to hear the word with the proper beginning sounds; then tension is released as he lets his body move as directed.

Ease and familiarity with alphabetic sounds are vital steps toward understanding written and spoken language. This game, superb at fostering just that, is one the child rarely tires of.

Touch the Line

Players: One adult, one or more children (older children play this by themselves)

The Game: Depending on which part of the child's anatomy is chosen, this game can be simple or exceedingly difficult. The parent makes a big circle on the floor with string or masking tape and, to start, asks the child if he can trace the circle with the tip of one shoe (this would involve hopping on one foot, while the other foot traces the circle) or if he can trace the circle with his hand always touching the line (this involves bending over and walking backwards as one hand traces the circle).

Variation: The game can proceed from the sublime to the ridiculous if the child decides that he will trace the circle with his ear, nose, or knee always touching the line; or the child or the parent can challenge each other by saying, "I bet Dad can't walk the circle with his elbow touching the line." (He probably can't.)

Comment: The child learns to identify and use specific parts of his body and coordinate that knowledge with the specific motor skill involved. He also learns the art of contortion.

Charlie Over the Water

Players: Six or more children

The Game: Players form a circle, holding hands around the child who agrees or is chosen to be Charlie-in-the-Center. As they walk around, the players chant:

> Charlie over the water,
> Charlie over the sea,
> Charlie catch a blackbird,
> Can't catch me.

At the last word, all the players squat, but Charlie tries to tag one of them before they squat. If he succeeds, the tagged player becomes Charlie.

Comment: Charlie Over the Water involves a beginning understanding of rules and cooperation. This is a basic game calling for a set of mutually agreed-upon rules and the skill to switch roles from being a member of the walking circle to playing Charlie. It's important to note that Charlie isn't isolated; he is within his circle of friends until he is no longer Charlie. Then he is a member of the walking circle again.

TEAM/GROUP

4 YEAR OLDS

All Fours Backwards

Players: One adult, two or more children

The Game: This is a spirited race-in-reverse game. The parent should place start and finish lines a maximum of ten yards apart, but less than that for younger players. At the word "Go," the children who are lined up at the starting line get down on all fours and race backwards to the finish line. (Lines can be just a piece of string run across the floor or lawn.) There should be plenty of distance between the finish line and any object behind it so that no child races into anything by accident. Variation: When the child reaches the line opposite the starting line, he can turn around after touching that line and race backwards to the starting line.

Comment: This is a valuable game for a child of this age, particularly if crawling backwards is presented as something hard to do. Anything hard he can do enhances his sense of mastery. The game is so ridiculous that it eliminates the sense of competition, clearing the way for an unusual exercise in coordination. The child's aim is to make it backwards along the prescribed route. Winning is not as crucial as succeeding.

Shadow Tag

Players: Four or more children

The Game: The child chosen to be "It" tries to step on the shadow of another player, who becomes "It" if his shadow is stepped on. The point is to twist and dodge to avoid being caught.

Comment: "It" isn't hurting anyone by stepping on his shadow, but the child is given a fine outlet for his aggressions. The other players delight in the contortions they go through to outwit "It." Tension is dispelled by laughter when a shadow is caught, and built up again as roles change and the game begins anew. Children are also delighted to see the replication of their every movement on the floor or on the lawn. It is an affirming experience.

Potato Race

Players: Eight or more children

Materials: Potatoes and tablespoons

The Game: Children split into teams. Two baskets are placed at one end of the room (or lawn). For eight players, four potatoes are placed on the starting line and the race is run in relays. Using only the spoon, each player must pick up one potato and transport it to the basket. He returns it to the starting line and hands the spoon to the next relay runner. If the potato is dropped, the player must use only the spoon to pick it up.

Comment: Another introduction to the basics of team play is presented here in a game that tests the child's sense of balance.

Drive a Pig to Market

Players: Eight or more children

Materials: Two milk cartons or plastic bottles. Two wooden spoons with blunted ends, wrapped in a piece of cloth for safety.

The Game: Divide the children into two teams. Make a finish line at the opposite end of the room. The game is played in relay fashion with each team starting with one member. The object is to push bottles, using sticks only, to the finish line at the other side of the room and back to the starting point where the player hands the stick to the next member of his team.

Comment: This game is so silly that one wouldn't be likely to feel bad about losing it. But it establishes the principle of team play and, because it's a relay, it involves the expectations of others.

Duck, Duck, Goose

Players: Six or more children

The Game: Children form a circle sitting down. One child goes around the outside of it, tapping each child on the head while saying, "Duck, duck, duck, duck, duck, goose." ("Goose" is the last child in the circle.) Goose immediately springs up and starts chasing "It" (the tapper) around the circle, trying to catch him before he reaches Goose's former place. He usually doesn't catch him, so Goose becomes "It."

Comment: The directions make this sound like a mindless exercise, but this simple game has enormous appeal for the four-year-old. It has the value of being a group effort that teaches the child to take turns. As the child waits to become a "goose," tension is built up and then released. Since there's always the slight chance that "It" will catch Goose, the excitement is ever-present.

Musical Chairs: Variation I

Players: Eight or more children. Best for a large group of twenty to twenty-five children.

Materials: Chairs

The Game: Arrange chairs in a large circle using one less than the number of players. One child stands in the center without a chair. He picks a category and says, "Everybody with brown socks exchange chairs," then runs to sit in an empty chair. The child who is left standing is "It" the next time. Children are usually quick to pick out common denominators such as sneakers, shirts with buttons, blond hair, brown sweaters, etc.

Comment: It's always useful to draw children's attention to attributes they share with others. This contributes to the experience of bonding and helps protect against a sense of isolation and helplessness.

The time factor in this game creates a tension that challenges the child and provides much-needed exercise in control. It also illustrates that a "loser" in this game can end up in control of the game.

Introduction

5 YEAR OLDS

At five, the child is much less frantic about his vulnerability and feels less helpless, perhaps because he really is bigger and stronger and has mastered more skills.

No longer completely preoccupied with the need to feel some strength and solidity within his self, the five-year-old is better able to take notice of his peers. He now has more freedom to explore relationships and to learn how others like himself can in some ways increase his satisfaction, and in other ways threaten it. Those who add to his pleasure (most often by sharing it) become "best friends" and those who give him a hard time become enemies ("I hate him!"). Sometimes the same companion can switch from one role to the other with dizzying rapidity ("He's my best friend but now I hate him!").

The more mature five-year-olds who feel some confidence in their ability to hold friends begin to widen their sphere of social operation and relate to groups. ("Hey, Tom, you wanna belong to my club? I'm the treasurer and it costs ten cents.") This is the appropriate time to choose learning and skill-development games that are played with groups and teams. It's important to remember that soon this child will be a member of a class in grade school.

On with the Play

Players: One or more children

Materials: Old dresses, shoes, fake jewelry, scarves, turbans, hats, capes, furs—anything that is suited or can be adapted to the theme of the play the child is putting on is welcome.

The Game: A favorite TV show, book, or nursery rhyme are all grist for this mill. Often the child or children in concert make up the drama which they then stage and perform for an audience, usually Mommy and Daddy.

Comment: This is a variation of Let's Pretend. The essential distinction is the addition of an audience, which gives the child an opportunity to receive feedback on the subject of his self. The audience serves as a mirror, reflecting the child's self. In this game, the child presents himself to his audience in a role and in a fashion he expects to be pleasing. Crudely put, he's "showing off" in an acceptable manner, hoping for approval with which to feed his fragile ego. Fortunately, almost all parents know that the function of an audience is to applaud.

Still, some people are offended by the idea of applauding or praising something which they do not see as praiseworthy. They are missing the point. Children ask for approval of what they do. If they are doing something constructive, creative, and appropriate, shouldn't it be encouraged? A child will produce a play or a story or a picture as an expression of *his* vision, *his* mood, *his* stage of maturity. He's not entering it in a competition for its excellence to be judged by arbitrary standards. He's just saying, "Look! This is what I did!" And the appropriate response is "It's good (because you did it)!"

Let's Pretend

Players: One or more children

Materials: By the time he is five, the child is able to use whatever is at hand to play this game. He probably has a collection of old grown-up clothes to draw from and sometimes his imagination alone is the only prop he needs to play Let's Pretend.

The Game: At five, the Dress Up game can be expanded to Let's Pretend. The child assumes roles—he is Daddy or Mommy or Teacher or Dog or Cat, and he acts out a script of his own. Often this game starts when one child says to another, "Let's play house. You be the mommy and I'll be the daddy."

Comment: Here the child uses his imagination to explore how others might feel by assuming their roles. Putting himself in their place gives the child a much-needed opportunity to learn what to expect of others and is vital to the ultimate development of the capacity for sympathy and empathy.

Role playing is equally necessary in the development of the child's ability to deal with his own feelings. By stepping away from himself and assuming a role, he has an opportunity to act out feelings that might be otherwise unacceptable.

Add-a-Line

Players: One adult, one or more children

The Game: The adult asks the child if he would like to help him tell a story. If the child does not offer to start the story, the adult can suggest a first sentence and explain it will be the child's turn to say the next sentence. Below is an example of such a dialogue. But here the adult was too eager to lead the story. (See comment.)

Adult: One day there was a big lion in the coat closet.

Child: I heard a big sound coming from the closet.

Adult: The lion was roaring, "I want to get out of here!"

Child: The lion was clawing at the door.

Adult: He clawed so hard he broke down the door and it fell down with a big bang.

Child: And the lion got out and he went upstairs.

Adult: And he said, "I'm all tired out from that closet. I think I'll take a nap."

Child: And he got into my daddy's bed.

Adult: But then Daddy came home.

Child: And he saw the lion in his bed.

Adult: And he was—

Child: Mad. He told the lion to get out of there and go home.

Adult: But the lion roared, "No," and rolled over and started to snore.

Child: But Daddy dragged him out of bed and took him to his zoo.

continued

Comment: Ideally this game should allow the child to take the story in whatever direction his immediate concerns dictate. It requires some artistry on the part of the adult to be sensitive to the child's direction and emphasis so that he can plan sentences that will reinforce the child's use of the game to serve his immediate emotional needs.

For example, the adult should be aware that starting the game with the sentence "There's a lion in the closet," presents the child with a concrete situation, namely that there is a danger present and only the closet door protects him. Notice in the example above that the adult is much more eager to let the lion out than the child is. Since the adult insists on letting the lion out, this child was ingenious enough to send him upstairs. It's perfectly possible that another child might have been too frightened to think clearly and could have become panicky when the adult exposed him to the released beast. It seems to us that, with most children, it would be best to start this game with a more neutral sentence, thus allowing the child more scope to guide the story. For instance:

Adult: I've been looking at that coat closet and sometimes closets have very interesting things in them.

Child: I hear a big noise coming from the closet.

Adult: That may mean that something besides coats is in that closet.

Child: I think there is a big lion in there.

My Pet Dinosaur

Players: One adult, one child

The Game: Ask the child, "If you were able to pick anything you want for a pet, what would you choose?" If he says, "A pet dinosaur," ask, "What would you call him? Where would he sleep? What would you feed him? Where would he go to school? What kind of clothes would he wear? What games would he play?" Invite the child to take his pet with him to the greengrocer or supermarket, the park or museum. The child may continue to share information about his pet's habits, interests, idiosyncrasies, likes, dislikes, fears, and hopes. The adult can then continue to inquire about the pet's needs, adaptation to house living, and adventures. He might also further wonder with the child about, for example, how the rest of the customers would feel about having a pet dinosaur sitting at the table next to theirs in an exclusive and expensive restaurant.

Comment: Besides being great fun and a foolproof antidote for aloneness, this game provides the child with a means for coping with helplessness. His inadequacies can be compensated for, frustrations overcome, and emotions can find an outlet. If, for instance, one feels constrained in public restaurants, one can depend on the dinosaur to be uninhibited.

I'm-in-a-Book

Players: One adult, one child

Materials: A notebook with hard covers, filled with unlined paper. Glue. Envelope to be attached to one cover. Small (three by five inches) cards to fit inside envelope. Pencils.

The Game: Glue an envelope to one cover of the notebook. The child draws a picture of himself and is then asked for a simple statement describing the picture, e.g., What color hair do you have? The child may reply, I have brown hair. The parent records this below the picture and, in addition, writes each word on a small card— I have brown hair. The next time the child plays the game, he may draw a picture of himself with a dog and dictate, I have a dog. The parent adds a and dog cards to the collection in the envelope. Eventually, the child can take a whole collection of word cards out of the envelope and place each word on top of the matching word in each of his stories.

Comment: This game helps a child build his sight vocabulary. He also develops the ability to guess words he does not recognize through contextual clues.

This game helps the child get together with his self, pin it down, and put it between covers. By connecting his self with possessions, and physical attributes, etc., the child develops a reassuring sense of the self's reality and loses some of the tenuousness and fragility that make young children more vulnerable.

What's Next?

Players: One adult, one or more children

Materials: See below.

The Game: Draw the first four figures on lined paper and ask the child to finish the lines in accordance with the beginning pattern. The examples below should be three times their size. It discourages the child to work on something smaller than he can handle.

Comment: The figures should be simple geometric shapes and/or letters with widely spaced lines. These figures need to be large enough for the child to reproduce. Most five-year-olds have pretty good small-muscle control but, since neuromuscular development proceeds unevenly, there is no point in creating challenges that are beyond the child's ability. The purpose of this game is to develop visual discrimination and the concept of patterns. Visual-discrimination practice will make it easier to learn to read. Pattern recognition—organizing shapes into groups or families—is also useful in learning word skills but may be even more important in the development of logical thinking. There is logic in this game. (If y always follows x, the x always has to have a y after it.)

Lotto Small Letters

Players: One adult, one or more children

Materials: See page 68 for instructions on how to make a lotto board. Substitute small letters for large ones on the cards but continue to use capital letters on the lotto board itself.

The Game: The child matches the small letters on the cards to the large ones on the board.

Lotto Colors

Players: One adult, one or more children

Materials: See page 70 for instructions on how to make the Lotto Color Board, but this time instead of coloring the squares write the word "Red" in *black* ink on the board in capital letters. Then, in small letters with *colored* pencil write each of the colors on the cards. Use a red pencil for the color red, blue for blue, and so on. Later, use just black pencil for the cards.

The Game: The child matches the small letters on the cards to the words written in black ink on the lotto board. In the more advanced game he matches the colors also written in black ink on the cards to the lotto board.

Comment: This learning-to-read game is useful in helping the child learn two visual alphabets that correspond to one auditory alphabet. This is complex and confusing unless the learning process is broken down into components and each component related to each other, piece by piece. It's quite important that this be done in a way that's fun and that the games proceed in pace with what the child is able to take in. Rushing the learning process will confuse the lesson at hand.

Complete-a-Shape

Players: One adult, one or more children

Materials: See below for sample designs. However, the actual shapes should be three times larger so that they are easier to work with.

The Game: Ask the child to make the second shape look like the first one.

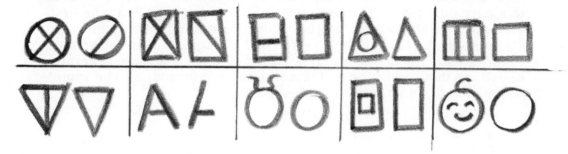

Which One Is Different?
Variation on above

Players: One adult, one or more children

The Game: Find the figure that is different.

□□I□ / AΔΔΔ / XXXL / MMИM

Comment: These figures can be made to require a higher and higher degree of visual discrimination. The child should be started on simpler tasks, and as the adult notices the child's increasing ability to pinpoint the solution, the problems can increase in difficulty. The games should be difficult enough to make triumph rewarding but not so difficult that frustration spoils the fun. Creating variations of this game can be addictive for vulnerable adults (who will know they are in danger when the figures begin to appear in dreams).

Twenty Questions
Animal, Vegetable, Mineral

Players: One adult, one or more children. (Ideal to play with both parents. One parent helps the child with questions.)

The Game: The game begins with a parent saying, "I am thinking of a [vegetable, animal, or mineral]." The child may ask twenty questions that have only yes or no answers to find out what it is. When he first starts playing this game, the child asks questions that are random guesses—Is it a tiger? A bear?—but as he progresses he learns not to throw away his chances and begins instead to ask more general questions that will in the end give him more information. The sample below includes sophisticated questions.

I am thinking of an animal.
Q. Does it live on land?
A. Yes.
Q. Does it fly?
A. No.
Q. Is it as big as a car? [Rather than "Is it big?" which is asked in the beginning stages.]
A. No. But it is almost as big as a very little car. [The answers are supposedly confined to yes or no but can be qualified when necessary.]
Q. Can I see it on the farm?
A. No.
Q. In the zoo?
A. In some zoos but not in all of them.
Q. Does it have spots?
A. No.
Q. Is it on the endangered species list? [Since a five-year-old is not likely to know the endangered species list, this question is apt to be suggested by a helping parent who explains.]
A. Yes.
Q. Can it hurt you? [Will it bite?]
A. Yes.
Q. Is it a panda?
A. Yes.

Comment: This is an exercise in logical thinking. It encourages the child to first think in generalities and then, slowly, in specifics, as a means of zeroing in on a solution. It provides practice in the logical process of hierarchical classification proceeding from group to subgroup to sub-subgroup. The basic procedure is progressive elimination. The ability to organize factual knowledge in a systematic fashion is a fundamental learning skill, perhaps *the* fundamental learning skill for acquiring facts. Five-year-olds have a relatively limited number of facts at their disposal and only very crude means for organizing these facts, but it's important to remember that in this game, it's the process that's important. What about the rare but occasional child who very quickly, by no detectable process of logic, consistently guesses what Mommy has in mind? Perhaps that child "knows" something at least as important as logic.

Buzz!

Players: One adult, one or more children

The Game: The parent asks the child to pick a number between one and ten. Then the parent asks the child to count to a hundred and tells him that each time the agreed-upon number or any *pair* of numbers containing the chosen number is reached, he should say, "*buzz!*" instead of the number. For instance, if three is chosen, the child should count, "one, two, *buzz*, four, five, six, seven, eight, nine, ten, eleven, twelve, *buzz*, fourteen, fifteen," etc.
Variation: This game can be a lot of fun with several children. Have them sit in a circle and say the numbers from one to a hundred in sequence, substituting "*buzz!*" each time they reach the number (or numbers-within-a-number) chosen by the group.

Comment: This game requires knowing number sequence, though certainly by the time it's over most children who haven't been too sure of their counting abilities will be far more confident. It can get hilarious if the numbers are said quickly. When it's played with several children, the faster the children go the louder the game seems to get, until sometimes it gets so fast and loud the players can't keep up!

Card Match Game

Players: One adult, one or more children

Materials: Deck of cards.

The Game: Use half a deck of cards—one red suit and one black suit. Spread out the cards at random, face down in three or four rows. The first person to play picks up a card and leaves it face up in front of his place. He then picks up one more card. If it matches and the number is the same (i.e., a five of clubs matches a five of hearts), the player keeps it and turns both cards face down in front of his place at the table. He is then entitled to another turn. If it does not match, the player puts it back exactly where he found it. It is now the next player's turn.

Each player's memory skill is tested since the object of the game is for each player to remember the number and the placement of the rejected cards so that when his turn comes and, for example, he has drawn a six that another player has turned back, he can immediately pluck the matching six from the row on the table. The winner of the game is the player who has picked up the most pairs.

Comment: This is a simplified variant of the game called Concentration. Success depends entirely on the child's ability to memorize the value and location of the briefly exposed cards. The skill involved is the sustained focusing of attention.

There is tremendous variability in this skill and the same child's ability can fluctuate from day to day and even *during* the game. All sorts of distracting influences can affect performance. Here again is a game where a five-year-old might occasionally give an adult some surprisingly stiff competition.

The Grid Game

Players: One adult, one or more children

Materials: Paper, pencil for an adult to make up grids. Grids are often found in daily newspapers but may be too complex for children.

The Game: This is a find-the-words game that can be made with a varying number of letters. Each "word scramble" has a theme. The player is told that there are many words relating to this theme in the letter grid. He should look up and down, across, and diagonally to find them. See samples. Note: The number of letters should always be the same or equal on all sides.

What do you put on your feet?

What's in the barn?

What animals do you see in the zoo?

Comment: This game involves word and letter recognition. A child gets the same sense of gratification from completing the above grids as an adult does from finishing a crossword puzzle. But this is fun only for the child who knows how to spell quite a few words much in the same way that crossword puzzles are fun only for adults when they feel they have a fighting chance. The child who is only familiar with capital letters cannot solve these grids if they are presented in lower case. Nor will he have an easy time if he's a shaky reader, and if the grid is too big and filled with words that are too long.

The challenge must be a reasonable one, both at first glance and upon doing. Naturally, the puzzles can get increasingly more difficult, but only in accordance with the child's abilities.

Touch and Recognize

Players: One adult, two or more chidren

Materials: Five objects such as a potato, piece of string, button, banana, mushroom, tomato, piece of macaroni, paper clip, roll of tape, hard-boiled egg, etc.

The Game: Players sit in a line with blindfolds on or in a darkened room and pass objects along down the line. The object is then hidden by the adult and when the blindfolds are off, each player tries to guess what he has felt.

Comment: It's tempting to play games that stress visual discrimination because we know it's useful in helping children develop reading readiness and reading skills. This kind of game, played with blindfolds, reminds us not to neglect sensory discrimination. Development in this and other areas is important. The game described above can be adapted for taste, hearing, and smell. All are fun, and if familiar objects are chosen, the adult is likely to find that in some areas the child does better than the adult. The child, whose parent is always teaching him, will get pleasure from occasionally putting that parent in his place.

The Blooper Game

Players: One adult, one or more children

Materials: Made-up story with blanks. Small slips of paper. Pencil.

The Game: Ask the child or children (depending on the number of blanks) to name a number of objects in these categories: furniture, kitchenware, food, clothes, and animals. Write these objects' names on blank pieces of paper and distribute them to each child. Explain that you will start reading the story to them and will come to spaces or blanks that you want the child to fill in. His job is to find the silliest (most inappropriate) word among those in his collection and read it. (Sometimes a child may need help reading a word.) For example, if a sentence reads, "My mother got out of her _____ this morning and walked inside her _____," the two most ill-fitting and therefore funniest words the child could find might make the sentence read, "My mother got out of her book this morning and walked inside her broom."

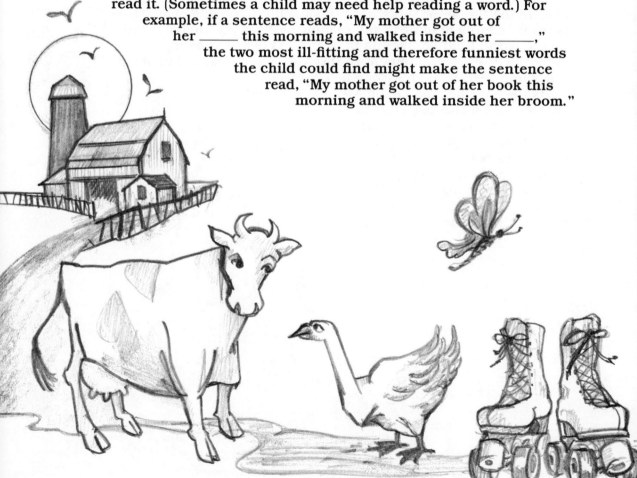

The following sample story has twenty-five blanks.

Poor Annie

Annie was a crazy cow who often didn't know what she was doing. Early one morning she rose and walked out of the _____ into the _____. After that she was even more confused and she started eating a _____. Then she sat down on a _____. That made her jump up and hit a _____. From then on things went downhill and she saw a _____ that mysteriously turned into a _____. The next thing Annie encountered was a _____ coming home from work. She turned around and there was a _____ who said hello to her. She backed into a _____ and the _____ that was next to her began to cry.

Annie couldn't bear to hear anything cry so she ran up the _____ and jumped over the _____ but unfortunately she knocked over a _____. Then the _____ began to jump up and down and the _____ began to scream and pandemonium broke loose.

Meanwhile there was another _____ in the meadow. He started running toward the lake where there was a _____ who ran away and jumped into the lake. By this time Annie was very bewildered indeed and she started wading in the _____. But it didn't feel good. So she left the lake and started to eat _____. It tasted terrible. By now, Annie was very discouraged and asked a _____ for help. It was no help at all. She decided she had better go home but unfortunately she stepped on a _____ and it got very angry. Annie decided she was very tired so she lay down on a _____. It was not at all comfortable. Furthermore, the wind blew and shook a _____ off the tree above. Now Annie was determined to go home, and when she got there she found a _____. After that Annie took a long, long nap.

Comment: Bloopers make children crack up. This game gives them a chance to practice reading skills—hilariously. And it also, in an imaginative and spirited way, exercises a child's ability to classify and categorize. To pick the funniest option he has to choose what fits *least* well. Up until now most games which require these kinds of skills have asked the child to pick the item that fits the *best*.

Run Like a Thief

Players: One adult, one or more children

The Game: This is a game for parent and child to play on the way to school or market. The parent asks the child to do any of the following in any order:

Run in a circle
Run in slow motion
Run backwards
Run and clap
Run funny like a clown
Run fast like a thief
Run and freeze
Run with your feet out
Run with your arms spread
Run like a whirling top
Etc.

Comment: This is a game to enliven parent-child trips to school or to the market. We have included only one gait game for five-year-olds because most prefer to share such games with their peers. This one provides exercise in the disciplined control of large-muscle groups.

Beanbag Race

Players: Eight or more children

Materials: Two beanbags

The Game: Children form two teams, standing in lines opposite each other. The team who passes the beanbag from one end to the other and back again first, wins.

Comment: In this game the child can readily begin to identify with his team or team members. He sees their value for him and recognizes his own value for them. How will the losing team members deal with this demonstration of their inferiority? Will they accuse the winning team of cheating? Will they find a scapegoat on their team and say it's all *his* fault? Or will they have enough confidence in whatever strengths they have so that they can afford to accept the knowledge that they may also have limitations? How many of us have enough self-awareness to deal gracefully with failure and rejection? What will you teach your child about a person's worth?

Crusts and Crumbs

Players: Eight or more children

Materials: String and a wide-open space.

The Game: Players form two lines three or four feet apart, facing each other. One line is crusts, the other crumbs. Each line has a safety base, marked with a string about fifteen to twenty feet behind it. (If in a play yard with walls or convenient trees, use those as safety base.) The teacher or parent, rolling *R*'s to heighten suspense, calls, "Crrrusts," whereupon the crust line takes off for its safety base. The crumbs try to catch the crusts before they reach their base and if the crumbs catch a crust, the crust becomes a crumb. The winning team is the one with the greatest number of players after a previously agreed-upon equal number of calls have been made for each team.

Comment: Team play is important when children are ready for it. Among many other things, it teaches the child the mutual dependency on which relationships are based. He learns to value the other fellow because the other fellow can help him get something he wants. He learns that he is valued because he can help the other fellow. When people get together to work for a common end they develop a regard for each other and the group. This is loyalty, and it is this that is at the core of Crusts and Crumbs. Players will find themselves having to switch loyalties several times during the game, in order to work with their current team.

Musical Chairs II

Players: One adult, eight or more children

Materials: Straight chairs. Record player or piano (and piano player).

The Game: This old-timer remains a favorite. The object is to have the children walk around a row of chairs that has one less chair than the number of children; for eight children, use seven chairs. Arrange the chairs so that every other chair faces in the opposite direction. The minute the music begins, the children start walking, *not* running, around the chairs. The second it stops the children fortunate enough to be in front of a chair sit. The child who is stuck in between chairs or at the end of a row is "out." When two bodies land on the same chair, it's up to the parent to arbitrate. Before the next go-round, one chair is removed and then the music begins again. Finally, two players and one chair are left; tension increases unbearably as the last two scramble around their lone chair until the music finally stops and the winner sits.

Comment: Before five, the child is not ready to face the perils of competition. It exposes him to the things he fears the most— isolation, humiliation, and damage to his self-image. A game where players are eliminated *one at a time* can make an excluded child burst into tears. Until the child has enough self-esteem, he should not be put into this position.

By the middle of the school year, cliques that are subject to constant reorganization have begun to form in the five-year-old group. Nicky and Tom will get together and tell Joey, "You can't play with us." If Joey is not crushed by this rejection, he may have the presence to look for someone who will accept him. Perhaps Janey will play with him. Anyway, half an hour later Nicky and Tom have split and are ready to take up Joey again. The important issue is that Joey is learning to deal with being left out from time to time. Today's child grows up in a society which measures people's worth and lets them know the score. Success and failure are key concepts and are marked by acceptance and rejection. We are trained for success, but success is relatively easy to accept. We need to learn better ways to deal with failure.

Musical Chairs is a good beginning competitive game because it goes fast and nobody is left out alone for very long.

Hopscotch or Potsy

Players: Two or more children

Materials: Concrete yard or street, white chalk, two or three keys on a ring.

The Game: 1. Players agree about the order of their turns, which remains the same for the duration of the game.

2. The first child to play stands in the rest space and throws the keys into square number 1. A bunch of old (no longer in use!) keys are best for this because, unlike a stone or other missile, keys won't jump into another space or square when they land.

3. If the child misses square 1, it is the next child's turn. Whenever a child misses his designated square—and bear in mind it is up to the individual player to keep track honestly of where he is in the game—he passes his turn to the next player and waits until his turn comes up again. His turn is also over if, in the process of the game, he steps on a line or into the wrong square.

4. As soon as the key lands in the proper space (number 1 to begin) the player hops from the rest space into square 2 *on one foot*; from there, he hops into 3 on the *same single foot* and then jumps into 4 and 5 using *both feet* (right foot on 5, left on 4), then into 6 on one foot, and finally 7 and 8 with both feet. At that point he *jumps around*, landing with his right foot on 7 and left on 8, hops into 6 on one foot, 4 and 5 on both, 3 on one, then hops into 2 on one foot, at which point he leans over and picks up the keys from square 1 and hops into the rest space using both feet. If he has jumped into each square in the proper order *without touching any of the lines*, he can continue to a second turn. He throws the keys into the box labeled 2 and begins again.

5. If a player has started, for instance, with square 2 and steps on a line halfway through the course, his turn is automatically over and he has to start again with square 2 the next time his turn comes up.

6. The game can be declared finished after the player has completed eight successful turns, or the players can go another eight turns by simply reversing the course. A very good player could conceivably complete the course on one turn, but that doesn't happen often with five-year-olds.

Comment: If you watch two four-year-olds struggling to play Potsy after you have seen it played by two five-year-olds, you will get a striking demonstration of the tremendous strides the five-year-old has made in a year. Two four-year-olds tried it the other day at a nursery. Instead of one set of keys, they had to have two. They approached the game like mad scientists, in dead earnest, but they made up rules as they went along and changed them constantly. The keys were thrown from a different place every time onto their design, which bore only a faint resemblance to a set of squares. They hopped onto the squares as erratically as they had thrown the keys and were quite pleased with themselves. "It's my turn" and "It's your turn" were said over and over, but they couldn't wait for either even though they could parrot the language well enough. The couldn't stick to the rules because they couldn't grasp the sequence but were satisfied by looking as though they were competently playing an older group's game.

At four the child can cooperate, but only in a very rudimentary way, because his expectation of the other child is so limited. At five he can understand, stick to rules, and is able to wait for his turn. The necessary adherence to sequential principles is within his grasp.

Tug of War

Players: Four or more children

Materials: Stout rope with a knot in the middle. Length depends on the number of players.

The Game: A central line is marked on the ground or a piece of string put down. The knot in the rope is placed over the central line. Players, divided evenly, stand on either side of the line holding the rope. At a signal they start trying to pull the other side over the central line.

Comment: Tug of War is the source of the phrase "pulling your weight." Clearly a value is set on the individual's maximum contribution to the group effort. The winning team has the members who have given their all, are the strongest, and/or who have the most weight.

Poor Pussy

Players: Four or more children

The Game: The child who is chosen to play "It" picks a victim from among the other children who stand around him in a circle. The objective is to make his victim laugh. "It" kneels and rubs against the victim, purring and mewing, saying over and over, "Poor pussy, poor pussy." If "It" laughs first, he has to move onto another target; if the target laughs, he becomes "It."

Comment: This is a big favorite and is multifaceted. It's ridiculous and great fun. And since it involves touching and tenderness, something meaningful to everyone, it's a warm game with no danger of derision.

Mastery and power are key issues here too. The child is totally gratified when he finds he has the power to induce laughter in others or the power to stop himself from laughing (but he never does for long). Hardly anything unites a group as much as shared laughter.

Blind Man's Guess

Players: Six or more children

The Game: Players form a circle with a blindfolded "It" in the center. "It" is turned around several times and then set loose to touch any of his playmates (who are asked to stand still). The touched player has to stand still while his face and body are being felt by "It," whose objective is to guess the player's identity. If "It" identifies the touched player correctly, that player becomes "It."

Comment: All blindfold games force the child to rely on means of orientation other than visual. Most such games emphasize tactile sensation, as this one does.

Blind Man's Guess can be varied by requiring the touched child to say "hello," and having "It" identify the touched player by voice.

Three-Legged Race

Players: Four or more children — eight would be better

Materials: Strips of old sheet to tie two children's (one each!) legs together.

The Game: This is played in teams if there are enough youngsters. Two children with two legs tied together race the length of the room, which has clearly marked start and finish lines.

Comment: We mused about the effect this game might have on the institution of marriage. Does the child learn that he who flies alone flies freer and faster? Or does he learn that since we're all hobbled, the most harmonious partners fare best? Children have more fun playing this game while adults have more fun thinking about it.

We consider this one of the most important children's games ever devised. Each child is very dependent on the other to make it through the race. They may have to alternate, compensating for each other's weaknesses or false steps. Sharing the same "obstacle" and goal encourages them to understand and have patience with the other's (lively) troubles! It should be played as soon as children are able and as often as possible—but not to the point that it ceases to be fun.

Blindfold Obstacle Race

Players: Four or more children

Materials: Fifteen feet or more of clear space or an outdoor lawn. Obstacles with curved or nonthreatening edges, such as cardboard cartons, cushions, wastebaskets, plastic bowls, empty suitcases, etc. Blindfolds. Two pieces of string for finish lines.

The Game: The child chosen to be "It" is blindfolded. His goal is to navigate his way through a "course" of obstacles that have been placed in zigzag fashion across approximately fifteen feet of space. "It" is allowed to take a long look at the arrangement of the objects before the blindfold is in place. When his eyes are covered, "It" starts out as the others watch and try and guide him through by shouting "yes" (meaning all clear) or "no" (meaning watch out, obstacle ahead). If "It" touches an object, he is led back to the beginning of the course and asked to start over. Each player gets two chances at trying the course.

Comment: Because it involves the beginning of real empathy, this is an excellent group game. The watching players shout with approval when "It" gets through the course and moan in sympathy when "It" touches something and has to start over.

This is similar to the Card Match Game (on page 105) in that it requires visual orientation and sustained focus of attention. But here the spatial orientation is three-dimensional. The visual deprivation is complete and the whole body must be manipulated within the restricted boundaries the child has tried to memorize before he was blindfolded. This is a much more physical game and involves the child in a more personal way. It is not truly a team game, since the contestants operate as individuals and the other players function not as a team but as an audience whose function, remember, is to applaud. But the applause, and the yeses or nos, do supply support. The child who is on his own through the course knows he is not in fact alone. He can hear and feel that everyone is behind him.

Kick the Can

Players: Six or more children

Materials: Empty can. Circle made of string, four feet in diameter.

The Game: One player (not the one chosen to be "It") kicks the can, which is inside the circle, as far as he can and immediately all the children run off and hide. "It" must retrieve the can, put it back in the circle, and close his eyes while counting out loud to a hundred before he can start searching. If he spies somebody, he calls out that player's name and that player is then caught and must stand in the circle. But another player can release him by rushing up unseen to "It" and kicking the can. This means "It" has to begin the whole process all over again. When a fair number of players have been caught "It" is reluctant to stray very far to find the missing players, since he is afraid someone may rush in and kick the can. (This game can be endless, so it is a good idea to place a time limit on how long the current "It" can remain in his role.)

Comment: This is a complex version of Hide and Seek. In social terms, a key factor is that those players who are not caught have an obligation to their less fortunate teammates. It is, in other words, not enough to hide successfully; to succeed one must expose oneself to risk in order to release a caught teammate. Another key factor is that a team of one is pitted against a team of many and stands some chance of winning as well as an excellent chance of achieving a stalemate.

The Confidence Walk

Note: Whether or not this game is played should depend more on level of fear, rather than age.

Players: One adult, one child

The Game: A child, accompanied by an adult (always, at first) or another child, is blindfolded and walks from one room to another, holding his companion's hand. No word is spoken. The kinesthetic drama is played out when the companion drops the blindfolded player's hand and walks close to but not touching the player.

Comment: When a child is blindfolded, the hair on the back of his neck may literally stand up. This game may stimulate a number of such atavistic responses (e.g., "sensing" the presence of someone close by).

In any blindfold game, the child learns to rely on senses other than visual. The first time The Confidence Walk is played it should be illustrated with two grownups and never done with a child until he asks to try it. Some children are frightened of being blindfolded and thus made even more helpless. In this case a conversation may go on between the leader and the child as they walk around until the child feels more comfortable.

The game's purpose is to build trust in relationships and, of course, trust in self or a sense of self-reliance. Sensing the presence of another person whom one cannot see is an exciting experience. An important thing to keep in mind, however, is that every child will have a slightly different reaction to this game. The game is potentially frightening. The child should never be asked to play it if he has any overwhelming feelings of fear.

The author, Gretchen Buchenholz, founded Merricat's Castle Nursery School in 1973. At that time, it was located in space rented from the Children's Aid Society and served thirteen children who met three mornings a week. In July of 1974, the school moved to the Community House of the Church of the Holy Trinity and within a year grew into a full day care center and kindergarten with over one hundred children enrolled.

The aim of Merricat's Castle Nursery School is to help each child develop his or her unique self to its optimum and to gain awareness of and confidence in that self. The school has received several awards from CUNY, an organization comprising the City Universities and community colleges of New York, for outstanding participation in education.

Gretchen Buchenholz is the Director of the Nursery and the mother of four children. She was born in New York City and is a graduate of Hunter College and Columbia University. She is currently on the faculty of LaGuardia Community College City University of New York and was the founder of a school for troubled high school and college students at the Psychiatric Treatment Center in New York City. Recently, she founded a Senior Citizen Lunch Club, a program for neglected teenagers, and two soup kitchens. She is a board member of the Food and Hunger Hotline, chairman of the Hunger Committee of the Coalition for the Homeless, and winner of the *New York Daily News* Woman of the Year award.